"With God, All Things are Possible!"

Copyright 2016
All rights reserved

ISBN 978-0-9983078-6-2
ISBN

All rights reserved. No part of this publication may be reproduced in any means, in any way, without the permission, in writing, from the copyright owner.
A product of SkookumBooks. Com 864 236 8058

Skookum Book's Charms

The beautiful butterfly, that graces our flowers and bushes, goes through a mysterious and magical change in becoming an adult! The Greeks believed each time a butterfly emerges from its cocoon, a new human soul is born! Legend has it that whispering a wish to a butterfly, then releasing it to carry the wish to heaven, will make the wish come true! Perhaps this is when they acquire little clouds on their wings. The butterfly is a symbol of fresh life, happiness, and joy! The "night butterfly", the moth, is attracted to a flame and light, just like our souls are attracted to heavenly truths!

Hummingbirds are active, beautiful additions to our gardens, who give us a sense of life, nature's beauty, and fresh life! These "flying jewels" flit from flower to flower picking up and delivering pollen, so that life can continue. It's the creature that opens the heart and shows the truth of beauty! It brings laughter and enjoyment and the magic of being alive! The hummingbird stands for spreading love and joy!

Dedication: This book is dedicated to our son, Robert, being our youngest, he was always close to my heart! He was such a patient little fellow, and so loyal to his big brothers. He brought us many memorable moments with his athletic skills in track. He had a beautiful voice, being in Flower Drum Song, Annie Get Your Gun, Oklahoma,
and Brigadoon! He was always a hard worker and player in every-thing he did, He entertained many people playing in the Hobo Band at Cedar Point, Sandusky, Ohio, and later joining the Ohio State Marching Band as a freshman! Those years were some of our most memorable experiences. He was a class act!

Acknowledgements: I am most grateful for the privilege I had in teaching my fourth graders at Madison Elementary, Sandusky, Ohio! I loved those years, I loved the kids, loved the staff, and loved the work! I have missed it every day since my retirement!

The Human Dilemma of the Young

The Scramble for Power, Approval, and Money!

"Ecclesiastes"

Betty Lou Rogers

Illustrated By
Jenison Hardin

King Solomon wanted to be useful and good,
He wished to be the wisest on earth,
This should have made life easy at best,
Because he had everything of worth!

But Solomon found all the wealth in the world,
Did not satisfy his many desires,
He had it all, he had the best,
But happiness still, was an absent guest!

He studied, taught, he judged and wrote,
Kings from other lands came to learn,
He gave advice and guidance true,
He understood life, and what to do!

With all his knowledge, he failed to take,
The advice he gave to others,
The older he grew, the more he knew,
If you want to be happy, you have to pursue!

As Solomon matured, he felt distress in his life,
It was filled with trouble, trials, and pain,
He hoped to spare his younger friends,
By sharing the knowledge he had gained!

He found that people made bad selections,
They didn't choose wisely or smart,
Don't pin your hopes on what does not last,
Possessions only become your junk of the past!

Don't stake your future on what fades away,
Like winning a game, or buying a car,
All these distractions will wither away,
But, building and improving lives will remain!

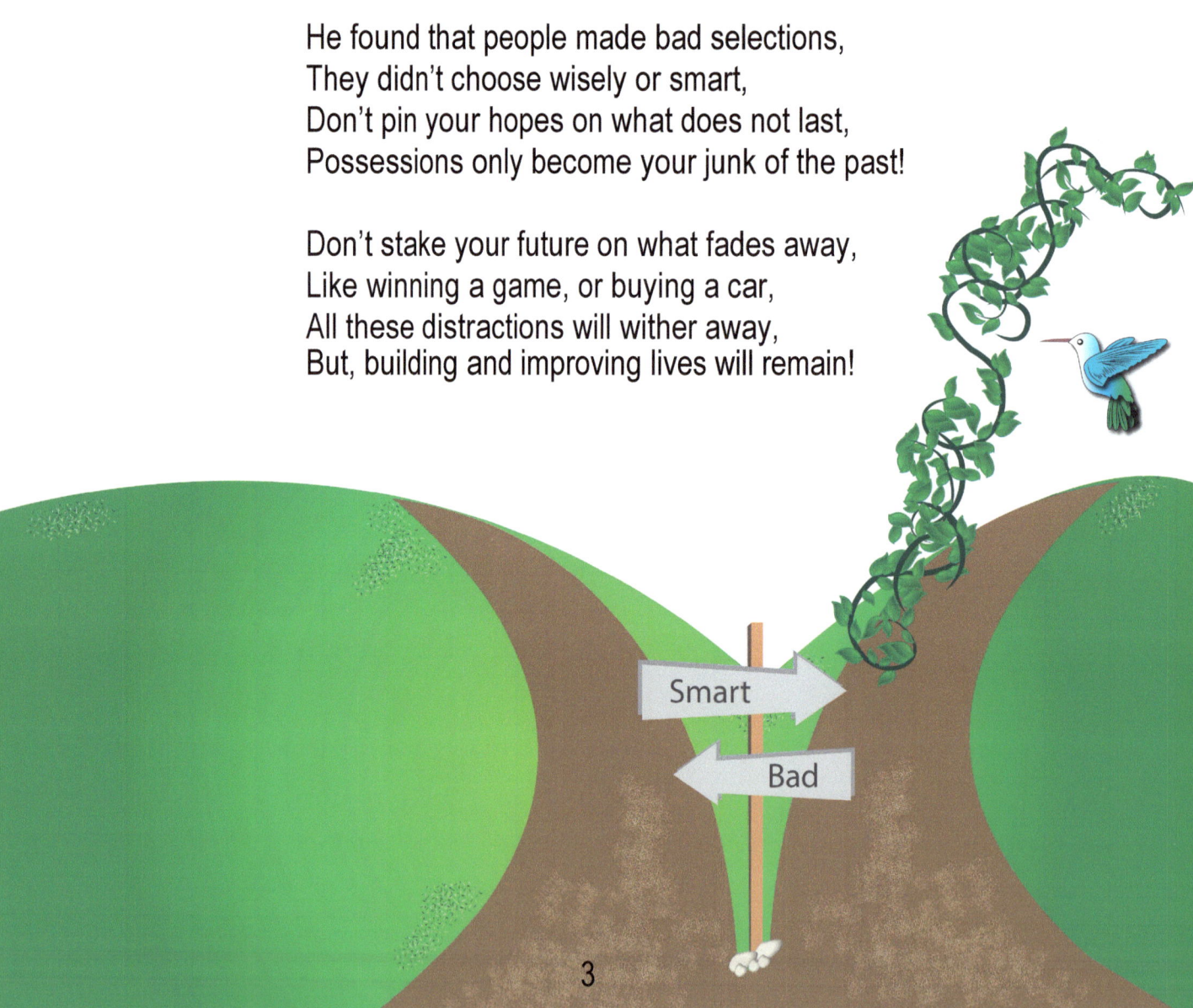

We're not here to serve ourselves,
But to tend and minister to others,
Commit to do what's good and fair,
Show that you really love and care!

Life is designed for togetherness,
We're not meant to live all alone,
We're meant to support, protect, and share,
To make every life better, beyond compare!

Solomon confessed it's hard to help,
Especially those who "know it all",
They don't want to listen or take sound advice,
So, they bring pain on selves, to be concise!

Solomon searched for a satisfied life,
For faith, fulfillment, and fun,
Focusing on passing pleasures is a waste,
Especially, if money and fame is your taste!

Solomon found we should treasure life,
Live it wisely, don't waste a day,
Fill up each hour with goodness you can do,
Because earthly pleasures won't do it for you!

Wisdom will save you from wicked men's ways,
They are weak, with evil thoughts and misdeeds,

You can direct your own life to whatever is good,
You can reap good results, by sowing the right seeds!

Much of the energy and work you exert,
Is useless, without reason, even foolish.
It's a waste of your time and so unwise,
To labor and live without God in your life!

How do you find good, valuable answers,
While keeping yourself out of trouble?
First of all, do everything proper,
And, for the right reasons, do them double!

Solomon feared the excitement of youth,
Might build up a wall, shutting God out,
He wanted the youth and their youthful ambition,
To make lives much better, improve the human condition!

Chasing the wind is a useless endeavor,
You can't see or know where it doth blow,
Faith is like the wind, moving about,
But you can feel it giving you hope, no doubt!

Wisdom grows with honor and respect,
It's being smart, and following good rules,
Working and playing hard, while treasuring life,
Living and loving, and avoiding all strife!

The wisest person can't understand God's ways,
For God has planned everything out,

He knows who we are, and what we can be,
It's signed, sealed, and delivered, for all to see!

Good Rules To Live By

Feeling guilty is not a good way to live,
Don't do things that you're sure to regret,
Be honest and truthful, with a grateful heart,
Knowing you're on the right track, is the best part!

Listen to the quiet words of the wise,
Pay no attention to the shouts of the fool,
Wisdom is better than weapons of war,
Be ready to curb vicious acts you abhor!

The heart of the wise inclines to the right,
The fool's heart leans to the left,
As the fool walks along, showing a lack of sense,
The height of stupidity is quite evident!

Be happy young man, while you are young,
May your life reward you with joy,
Just know you'll be judged for what you do,
Be wise, be true, it's all up to you!

Success is not always good,
Misfortune is not always bad,
If we live as God intends us to live,
We'll be content with whatever He gives!

Beware of being too righteous, too wise,
Don't be mislead by your own rigid rules,
God wants us balanced and whole in His eyes,
Seek true ways of living, and His goodness apply!

Those who think they're better than others,
Are often driven by envy and greed,
The "do nothing" idler, who sits on his hands,
Joins this other fool, neither much in demand!

People will be judged for what they do,
No excuses for doing what's wrong,
Human effort can't succeed all alone,
We all need God's guidance and help to be strong!

If you're looking for fun and enjoyment in life,
Through wealth, or power, or fame,
You might as well try chasing the wind,
Your life will be empty, just more of the same!

Our possessions are a gift from God,
They are there to be used, not revered,
They will not last, they're transient at best,
Good deeds have value, possessions much less!

Misfortune results from careless decisions,
It shows poor thinking, and dumb actions,
These people are weak, and puny in mind,
With this kind of behavior, there's no satisfaction!

Money talks, it can buy anything,
Bribes steal what belongs to the righteous,
Money pads the pockets of the foolish who lust,
These fools live a life, you never can trust!

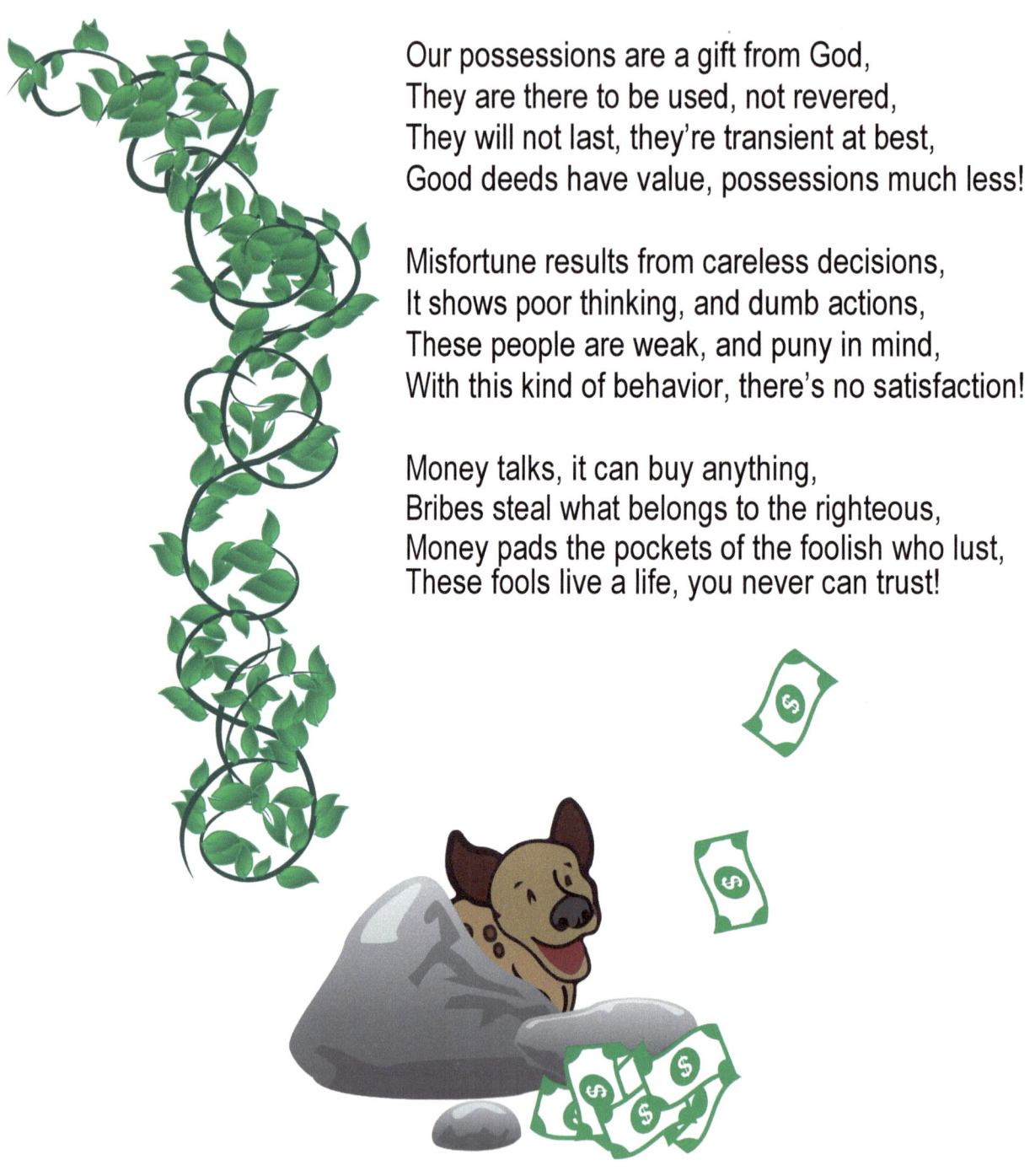

Love is doing, helping where you are needed,
Love is giving, your time, heart, and soul,
Love is living, showing others God's goodness,
Love is knowing and fulfilling your role!

King Solomon was so wise and smart,
He knew all the hazards of living,
He wanted to teach, advise, and the youth inform,
He wanted to save young people from other's scorn!

God has a plan for every soul,
You have to find His plan for you,
There is a right time to find your way,
To understand and accept what makes a good day!

Where will you find God's plan for you?
Not under a rock or in a deep hole,
You'll not find it in raindrops, or snowflakes so rare,
It's deep in your heart, waiting there, with care!

We'll never be satisfied with earthly quests,
Because we have spiritual needs,
Like being loved, accepted, and desired,
These free us to live, happily inspired!

There is a time and season for all,
A time to be silent, and a time to speak,
A time to tear down, and a time to build up,
Discover God's timing, for the life that you seek!

Animals and man are the same and not,
Neither lives forever, both come from dust,
When animals die, they stay dead that way,
Man has eternity, cause his heart's full of trust!

The lazy person doesn't care for success,
He won't work for himself, or his own,
Some people work for only greed and pride,
Both of these fools, need a much better guide!

The love of money can lead one astray,
Wealth, especially, attracts leeches and thieves,
When they die, no matter how much loot they collect,
Nothing goes with them, on this you can bet!

Trying to work without training and tools,
Is like using a dull ax to chop wood,
You'd do better to stop, and sharpen the ax,
And get the job easily done, as you should!

So, when you want to do a good job,
You must acquire the knowledge you need,
If you sharpen your skills, by learning real well,
Like that keen ax, you'll be sharp and excel!

When leaders think only of themselves,
They're unfit to lead, and will fail,
Whether they're selfish or lazy, decline will come,
A country with a raw, careless leader, will succumb!

There is true value in knowledge and work,
Also true of relationships and fun,
These traits have value when properly used,
And also when their worth is properly viewed!

Good times drive us toward comfort and calm,
Bad times, God allows, bring us to him,
He's in control, lets good things come through,
He wants us to accept the things that He'll do!

It is said every person has a price,
Except the wise man can not be bought,

But those who are unfair, dishonest, and cheat,
Are protecting corruptness, and full of deceit!

Life is a precious privilege we have,
To live, love, and enjoy what we do,
We should avoid evil and ungodly lives,
And, maintain a strong attitude of faith, without strife!

Good judgement is an important trait,
It might be unpleasant when first applied,
But staying on target, and moving ahead,
Toward eternal values that God will provide!

Do not steal is an important rule,
You might think taking a small thing okay,
But your angel inside is saying, "No no, No no"
Helping you remain honest, to your Father and you!

Beware of all the smooth talkers,
They are masters of deceit,
They can make any bad decision,
Sound like the best, most wonderful feat!

Watch out for the feeding frenzy,
Of those who love to take that pound of flesh,
They feed upon hurting those who oppose,
They're nurtured by the trouble they can provoke!

NEWSFLASH! Microphones aren't equipped with brains,
Good thinking must be supplied by the speaker,
There are those who don't seem to know this fact,
When they speak in a mike, it's clear what they lack!

A race isn't always won by the swift,
And wealth doesn't always come to the smart,
God does favor what you do with your life,
Your time and chance can be felt in your heart!

Beware of the talker, who is a master with words,
They can make murder sound good, and just right,
They will say anything, have no allegiance to the truth
So your brain has to work hard, make you very astute!

There are many people living today,
Who will swindle and cheat all they can,
Look out for them, and all their trash,
Tell them, "In God we trust, all others cash"!

So, what are passing pleasures?
It's wealth, and power, and fame,
Being selfish, dishonest, with evil desires,
Exhibiting childish behavior, such a shame!

Passing pleasures will finally fade away.
They disappear, having no value at all,
They do not comfort, enhance, or even cheer,
They are utterly forgotten, but much to fear!

If ever you want to make others feel worthy,
And show them you really do care,
Just light up your face with a sunny smile,
And send friendly greetings, to all, everywhere!

And if you grow weary, and full of doubt,
You want to be someone worth noting,
So, what do you do when you feel so defeated?
"Treat others the way you'd like to be treated"!

And always remember - - - Never forget:

America is your homeland,
'Twas won with blood and strife,
And cherish all your freedoms,
And guard them with your life!

About the Author

Betty Lou Rogers is a retired fourth grade teacher from Madison Elementary School in Sandusky, Ohio. Her strategy for success was simple. Engage! Work together! Be active learners! Then employ her "one more chance" philosophy

Betty Lou Rogers grew up in rural northwestern Ohio, graduating from Fremont Ross High School. She married her childhood sweetheart and raised three sons. During this time, she returned to college where she graduated with a B. S. Degree in Elementary Education from Bowling Green State University, in Bowling Green, Ohio. She was a member of the prestigious educational society, Kappa Delta Pi.

While teaching at Madison School, Mrs. Rogers was keenly aware of what children needed, both as a group, and as individuals, in effectual learning in the classroom! She also had the intuition to know how to accomplish this by being active learners, as opposed to the sit, listen, and absorb approach! Always have lesson material in front of the student, so they are actively participating in the lesson, never pushing the child beyond their ability, but always working toward the best they can do! Often times the student is awakened to and surprised by their own ability. Mrs. Rogers' most telling educational approach was offering the children "one more chance" to learn and succeed, by giving open-book tests!

Tests show what the student hasn't learned! "My job is to give the children every opportunity to learn." This strategy caused her students to become more familiar with the contents and location of information in their books. This offering, enabled them to find the answer, complete the test, and learn what was missed before! These answers could even be more meaningful to them! When parents found this out, there was no excuse for a failing grade!

Mrs. Rogers was also a Jennings Scholar, which honored and rewarded teachers in the elementary classroom. The Jennings Foundation provides a means for greater accomplishment on the part of teachers, with the hope it would result in greater recognition for those in the teaching profession within the public school system. Mrs. Rogers and her husband chose to retire in beautiful South Carolina. They are members of Advent United Methodist Church in Simpsonville, South Carolina! Besides writing, she loves her sewing and crafts, and gardening! Mrs. Rogers and her husband have four granddaughters, and seven great-grandchildren.

After twenty-seven years of teaching, Mrs. Rogers' philosophy for success has permeated the American landscape through her students in both academic and professional fields. Her love for teaching and writing, can never be equaled In any way, except for her hope for students to find her writing truly illuminating!

Mrs. Rogers published works:

The Thimseagle Thievers
Change Can Be Good
Paste and Gluey, A Sticky Tale
Kate Earns Her MBA in Manners. Behavior, Attitude!
Chris Earns His MBA in Manners, Behavior, Attitude!
It's So Important To Be Honest!
The Ten Commandments for Teens, and Helpful Hints In-Between!
Proverbs, The first Book Written For the Young, Plus A Little Bit For Everyone!
Acquiring The Human Skills of Thinking, Saying, Doing, For Teens!
USA, Democracy, The American Way!
A Medley of Options For The "Not Yet Old" Set!
Law and Order, Truth and Peace for Teens!
ABC's For Teens, and What They Mean!
Teens, Consider All Circumstances and Consequences!
Jealousy, It Will Chew You Up, Then, Spit You Out!
Loves Flowers, Hates Weeds!
So, You Think We Shouldn't Have Dropped "The Bomb?"
Bossy Susie Saucy
Capricious Caleb O'Connor
Mrs. Rogers' books are published under SkookumBooks.com 864 236 8058

www.ingramcontent.com/pod-product-compliance
Lightning Source LLC
Chambersburg PA
CBHW041231040426
42444CB00002B/128